Primal Reconnection

Primal Reconnection

"The Fundamental Missing Element in Our Modern Lives"

Tasha Sabatini

Primal Reconnection © 2016 Tasha Sabatini.

Check out my YouTube Channel at www.youtube.com/channel/TashaSabatini.

PLEASE READ

The content in this book reflects the author's (Tasha Sabatini) observations, experiences, and opinions on various topics and is in no way intended to replace a medical professional's advice.

All original artwork by Tasha Sabatini.
Photography by Tasha Sabatini and Michael J. Henderson, RecordedLight.com.

Table Of Contents

1 Primal Reconnection: What it's All About......1

2 I Just Like Being Outside.....................25

3 Fact or Fiction...................................28

4 Get Out...36

5 The Dying Breed.................................38

6 Wonders and Worries.........................53

7 Whole New View...............................59

8 Brighter Horizons..............................71

9 A 16 Year Old and The Natural World.........79

10 Bringing All The Elements Together...........84

Acknowledgments

To everyone young or old, family, friend, or stranger who has made an impact in my eventful 16 years here on this planet, my life would be much different without the guidance from all of you. I can truly say I would not be where I am today without your positive magnetism.

Thank you,

...especially to Madre, Mike, Emily, Mark, and Kyla.

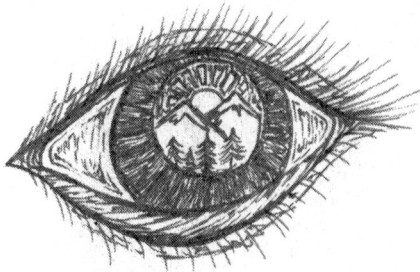

Chapter One

Primal Reconnection
and What it's All About

Have you ever seen something that truly, wholeheartedly takes your breath away?

I have.

I've seen a billion galaxies fade to a burning sun with my own two eyes from the comforts of a snow-covered hammock.

I've floated in a stormy ocean on a surfboard slightly bigger than myself. Ascending large waves and plunging back down deep below the horizon line...over and over again. Up, up, up, and down, down, down.

I have felt the sting of ice crystals hitting my face while snowboarding down a slope at ridiculous speeds. One slip up and you're tumbling down a hill like a rag doll, it's scary, but yet I have never been

more present, more in control of my own body than when I was on that slope. It is an amazing sensation.

I have found something that makes me feel alive. Have you?

What does reconnection truly mean?

I'd like to believe that we all know what the word "connection" means, but just in case let's analyze it a little closer.

con·nec·tion

[kə'nekSH(ə)n]

NOUN

1. a relationship in which a person, thing, or idea is linked or associated with something else:

2. "the connections between social attitudes and productivity" ·

3. [more]

4. *synonyms:* link · relationship · relation · interconnection ·

5. [more]

Okay, a relationship between you and something else, that's what a connection is. We've ALL had somewhat of a connection with something at least once in our lives. So we all understand how close we can become to that connection, whether it be a person, a thing, or an idea.

But what about reconnection? Is there a difference? Other than just the prefix "re"?

Yes, yes there is actually a difference between connection and reconnection. It goes like this: in order for reconnection to occur you would have had to have lost the original connection.

Of course, when we lose something, it's missing.

What the vast majority of people are missing is the essential, even crucial, element of including and incorporating the outdoors in our daily lives. We've slowly but surely lost this connection between humans and the outdoors. Not on purpose, but out of sheer modernization and other stimulus in this world. We spend our days clinging to our phones, our televisions, and our computers.

"ALL THAT IS **GOLD** DOES NOT GLITTER,
NOT ALL THOSE WHO **WANDER** ARE LOST;
THE OLD THAT IS STRONG DOES **NOT WITHER**,
DEEP ROOTS ARE NOT REACHED BY THE FROST"

— J.R.R. Tolkien

Random Fact, we are connected to this earth in even the strangest of ways. Elements on the periodic table such as gold are naturally occurring in the human body. We have about 0.000021 lbs of gold in us. Yes, it's a miniscule amount but it's still there, still naturally occurring in us and in nature.

We have exchanged new high-tech connections for our traditional and natural "walk in the park" and the "mud between our toes."

What's missing is the connection, and the element is the natural world.

I am seeking to evangelize the process of reconnection. Bringing back what we've lost and reconnecting any soul in the world that is willing to find greater purpose and better clarity, which is best obtained from the outdoors. It's a place of peace. It's a place where one can find passion and tranquility all at the same time.

I want everyone to know the feeling of standing on a mountain top looking out over a vast landscape. In that moment the world seems distant, but you can feel present. I've had periods where if I look at a computer screen or technology of any sorts for that matter, I'll start to feel nothing. I know I'm not the only one who has experienced this kind of perception and yet that is becoming reality while what's right around us is becoming fantasy.

We can't let this happen to us.

Don't you want to feel alive? Don't you want to sense every little detail you can with the time that we are given here on this earth?

Reconnection is the single most vital action you can take to experience living at it's highest ubiety. (look it up)

What does Primal truly mean?

We humans as a species are mammals, and mammals are technically animals... so in a sense we all have that animal instinct in us. Or, as I like to call it, a primal instinct.

in·stinct
NOUN
1. an innate, typically fixed pattern of behavior in animals in response to certain stimuli:
2. "birds have an instinct to build nests" ·
3. [more]

ADJECTIVE
1. formal
2. (instinct with)
3. imbued or filled with (a quality, especially a desirable one):
4. "these canvases are instinct with passion"

I find it very curious that in both utilizations of the word *'instinct,'* whether it's being used as a noun or an adjective, it is still applicable to both you and myself.

The primal part comes into play when it is used as a noun: Innate, fixed pattern of behavior, in response to, stimuli. We, as humans, have an instinct to wander into the woods, mountains, or oceans. It's in all of us, you could deny it, and some do, very well I might add. But at the heart of all of us that instinct is instilled, it thrives and a certain smell, sight, or touch can trigger a stimulant in our bodies.

That desire to be outside in the most natural of places is soon pulled through all those layers of modernism in us. *We crave the natural world.* That instinct is there, it's always there deep down waiting for that first sight of fresh snow, that first plunge into a frothing river.

That instinct is a primal calling within.

We are filled with it, to use instinct as adjective.

So let's take a look at primal again?

pri·mal
[ˈprīməl]
ADJECTIVE
  1. essential; fundamental:
  2. "for me, writing is a primal urge"
  3. *synonyms:* basic · fundamental · essential · elemental · vital ·
  4. [more] psychology of, relating to, or denoting the needs, fears, or behavior that are postulated (especially in Freudian theory) to form the origins of emotional life: See also primal scene. "...he preys on people's primal fears"

Primal. God, I love this word. Don't you? It's powerful, raw, and yet, simplistic. Translated across multiple languages and yet still retains the same meaning throughout, it's universal.

It's universal because people like you and I gravitate towards being in a primal state. It's a necessity to our overall survival and well-being. We

8

are primal beings, our lives are bona fide by what we think, how we act, whom we drift towards. Even in mental states of non-thinking, primalness is the single factor that keeps us going.

It's the lionheart inside.

So how do they relate to each other?

Primal. Reconnection. Together they create a very old and ancient custom. One not completely lost, but sure getting there.

Throughout our species' entire existence we have been outdoors. We hunted and gathered, we foraged and gardened, and we lived off the land. We embraced the elements, we told stories based on animal kind, in every ethnic group and origin around the world. From the continent of Australia to the Persian Gulf to The Isthmus of Panama to The Bering Strait and everywhere in between, above, and below.

May we embrace our Primal sides and Reconnect with what matters.

> "There are no random acts. We are all connected. You can no more separate one life from another than you can separate a breeze from the wind."
> - **Mitch Albom**

Story time…

On a recent Thanksgiving trip I took to the Outer Banks of North Carolina I experienced something unlike anything I have ever seen.

Could you imagine looking up at the stars over a wild ocean and then looking down at your feet in the sand surrounded by the same glowing you saw looking at the sky?

Strange huh? Very. But also completely amazing.

Noctiluca is a large dinoflagellate. It's a bioluminescent algae essentially.

It was unreal, a few of us had gone out to one of the most secluded parts of the Island that we could access. The stars were about the brightest I had ever seen. In front of me was the Atlantic Ocean just completely roaring, and yet peaceful at the same time. At some point within the first 10 minutes of being there with all our eyes locked at the sky, one of us happened to look down at our feet and notice a million little lights glow for just a split second in the sand.

It was the Noctiluca making the sand sparkle every time we took a hard step or shuffled our feet. That's just what we all did too, for a good 45 minutes if I might add. It wasn't a very warm night, either! Our 5 minute trip to look at some stars turned into over an hour of us stomping around, eyes locked between our feet and then over our heads. It was like being in between two mirrors. You look at the sky and you would seen a billion tiny white lights, you would look at your feet and see the same thing.

We even made sand angels, which were truly spectacular when mixed with all the Noctiluca!

It was both unreal, and yet, the most real phenomenon one can experience.

Disconnecting and Reconnecting

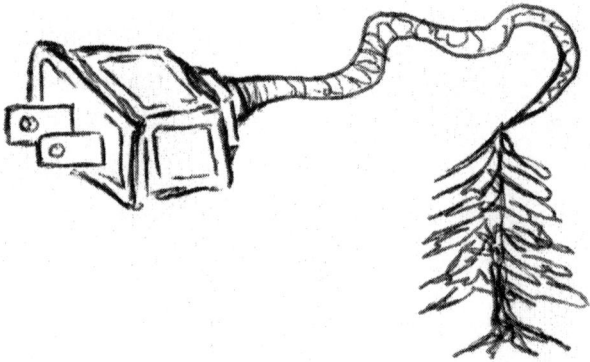

With technology literally at my fingertips it's so easy to get enthralled with the accessibility to it, and while it isn't all bad by any means, because I'm making use of it to reach people and connect with them, there is a fine line, however, between use and overuse.

We as a people are replacing natural reality with virtual realities.

"Real freedom lies in wilderness not in civilization."
    - Charles Lindbergh

We are connected to a screen of some sort almost twenty-four seven. I have found times where

12

I go to interact over a social media platform thinking to be on there just for a quick check-in and then an hour goes by within what seems a minute.

It consumes us.

We find "peace" while binging on TV series for a days at a time. We feel better connected now that within a few seconds we can interact with the entire world through a phone/computer. We believe we're ultimately okay with just being engrossed by all that modern technology has to offer us, but the truth is, that is no way for us to live.

Losing ourselves in a virtual world and looking past what is naturally occuring around us is a huge downfall that is affecting us both physically and mentally.

Technology has been directly linked to health problems of all sorts. When you spend at the least six hours a day connected to a phone, watching TV or scrolling online, the consequences become more apparent. For example, we observe how animals in captivity function completely differently from their counterparts in the natural world, and we work so hard to provide freedom and better, more natural conditions for animals in captivity. We are saddened when we watch the captive lions and tigers pacing in their caged displays, or the otters that only have 10-square feet of water and land to swim in; so why does this not apply to us humans?

We shouldn't be in captivity; it's not how we're wired. Technology subdues us with invisible fetters and chains that are unnatural restraints. It's so important for us to disconnect from our devices, I cannot stress this situation enough! Reasons such as loss of sleep, which then changes one's mood/ mindset overall changing how they interact; behaviour and physical problems are surfacing, such as structural issues in our body, along with radiation that all our devices put off, are leading to untold effects on all of us.

The main point is disconnecting, but why?

Why should we eat better? Because it's good for us, just like disconnecting is good for us.

Ahh reconnection. Yes, again reconnecting with the outdoors, if you haven't caught on by now. Reconnecting with the trees, the rivers, the mountains, and the oceans, and disconnecting with the smartphones, the computers, and the TV's.

My suggestions for closing out of the phone...

Ahh yes, the inevitably dominating cell phone.

There is no disputing that just about everyone has a phone, it is 2016 after all. We like our phones, we like them a lot; perhaps a little too much for our own good.

Some people do just fine checking their phone once a day and calling it good, but I know all too well how rare that behaviour is. At the end of the day phones are a legitimate addiction.

ad·dic·tion

[ə'dikSH(ə)n]

NOUN

1. the fact or condition of being addicted to a particular substance, thing, or activity:
2. "he committed the theft to finance his drug addiction" ·
3. "an addiction to gambling"
4. *synonyms:* dependency · dependence · habit · problem

How about that, an addiction is a dependency, a habit, and most importantly, a problem.

The first step to fixing a problem, of course, is admitting there is one. We as a culture must admit that the modern addiction to our phones is a huge problem.

We are missing out on life.

Just the other day I was lifeguarding at my high school's pool when one of the most apparent realizations hit me like a Mack truck. Yes, the phone addiction is all too real. It was a Wednesday night swim for the college students in my town provided by the University. But how I've always seen it, was as a way to hang out with my other friend who'd lifeguard it with me and do homework. No one ever came to these evening swims, and I'd get paid to sit there, really, I had no qualms about it either. Occasionally, we'd have a YMCA swim coach stay and swim but it was usually right at the beginning and they were done pretty fast. This particular night was exactly that.

Both of the YMCA swim coaches stopped in to swim, and along with them was one of their sons and a fellow swimmer. They are the types to get their workout done and get it done well, so it was totally fine they did their thing and all was good.

Then for the first time ever a college student came in to swim actually. My friend who was guarding with me looked over at me with the same expression that I know was on my face too. The guy came in, headphones on, face in his phone, and then disappeared into the locker room. He emerged quite a while later but with jammers on, so we figured he was legit (Jammers are what guys wear for sport swimming). That he would just pound out the laps like swimmers do, well, we thought wrong.

He proceeded to walk over to the far side of the pool, and then he sat on the ladder with his feet in the water for a bit. What we then noticed was that he had his phone with him, not only did he have his phone with him, but he was on it for some time and that's when my friend and I realized that he was Snapchatting people.

For those of you who might not know exactly what Snapchat is, it's a photo/video sharing app that lets you send pictures of what you're doing, where you are at, and when, and whoever you send these to can only view it for 10 seconds. A true Millennial paradigm (I use it too, so I haven't got room to talk).

Anyways, after a few minutes of this he then hops into the pool, **phone in hand** (what the heck??) and continues to take pictures of himself while in the pool!

Why, I'd never seen anything quite like it before! That isn't the end of the story though, it just got stranger.

He put the phone down, finally, on the edge of the pool and then started into a lap. Well, the second he went under and took one stroke of freestyle, he came back up to his feet again, then walked back over to his phone and checked it for a total of 5 seconds. Set it down again and did one full length of the pool after all this, caught his breath for 3 minutes and then swam back to where his phone was. This cycle repeated itself for about 5 more times over a period of 40 minutes. When he was obviously done with his "laps" the guy just stood in the water, phone in hand, taking pictures of himself. He'd try and set it down for a minute at a time, but then would get fidgety and go and pick it back up again. It was a true spectacle. Sheesh!

At first my whole opinion on the situation was like, "you do you buddy," but after so long it became funny, and then just disappointing.

I greatly respected the fact that one of the college students finally came to the pool, but that respect soon diminished as I realized he wasn't there to better himself actually.

It was the first time I really, truly, wholeheartedly realized the severity of the phone addiction that faces most people today. Even after getting out of the pool he didn't say one word to the two of us who were lifeguarding, and we usually interact with everyone who comes through into the natatorium. He walked in staring intently at his phone with headphones on, and he left just the same. No real human interaction on any part, at any time, outside of his phone.

That has to be about the saddest piece to it all. We are missing out on life.

Missing the physical connection between yourself and a loved one.

Missing the physical joys of being out and about, whether it be in the city or country.

Missing seeing awe-inspiring sights and not just on a 5.5 inch screen.

Missing hearing noises from afar and up close instead of from a measured amount of Hz within a phone.

Missing tasting that piece of fruit your friend ate and took a picture of to put on her Instagram.

Missing touching the hand of a person you love, instead of double tapping to like a picture of someone. These are real physical relations that we lose every time we choose to interact with our phone rather than the real, tangible world around us.

I'm not going to go off on a huge rant about how phones are destroying everything that is precious in life, but I would like to share a few ways to cut the addiction to your phone.

So we have a problem at hand, and we've established that.

But how do we fix it?

Mindfulness and effort.

Mindfulness comes into play big-time with this scenario. We become so consumed in our phones that our heads are fogged by it, 5 minutes turns into 2 hours real fast on a phone. That's where we have got to be mindful about our time spent on the phone. One of my best suggestions is to put the phone away from you when you absolutely know you don't need it. In the car, sleeping, eating, with friends and family are times when the phone is way better off in the pocket rather than in the hand.

Airplane Mode is your best friend.

If you can learn to just put your phone on airplane mode, you're golden. It will cut down that temptation by a lot. Nothing can light up the screen every 2 seconds when in airplane mode, it's great! What a concept! No 4g, LTE, wifi access, it's pretty awesome! Along with turning the phone to airplane mode you can also turn off notifications from some or all platforms if you'd like. That way you won't be opening your phone back up for every single notification about a Like or a spammy notification.

It's not easy to just go cold turkey on any form of addiction, whether a minor one or a major one it usually just sets you up for failure, and that's not the point of all this. It takes effort and self discipline, but that comes with achieving anything good worth achieving. Try and put yourself in the position of thinking that by putting the phone down more it will only benefit you, and it will.

The Phone Purge

Try this for a total of 2 days.

For day 1, go through your day how you normally would, but keep a tally of how many times you check/get on your phone.

On day 2, **go completely without your phone**.

Don't even have it on you, and **yes it's possible**. Most of you lived before the time when phones weren't mainstream, at one point in your life you did not have a phone on your person whatsoever.

I'm 16. and I still remember the time when I had no phone on me! (If you refuse this step then you're only hurting yourself, you've made up in your mind already that you won't face this problem and that you do not want to change up your life. That's fine, you do you, but you are obviously not ready to help yourself) Anyways, so yes, for one whole day no phone, just be present.

To make this step easier, it might help to actually go someplace where phone access is limited to none...yes, these places do exist! Go out into a very rural location or even a very lonely beach where there is just no phone service and immerse yourself in that environment.

In every possible way be present. Be so present you scare yourself. Pay attention to how you feel, how others feel.

. Do you feel pain?Joy? Whatever it is you feel, embrace it. Look at different faces and their expressions, their body language.

Look at the sky, anything different? Smell your shampoo. Taste your morning coffee for once. You might just realize all the life you've been missing out on as you carry on life in full-on distraction mode.

After the 2 days you can decide for yourself if this method helped you at all. My hope, of course, is that it does, and if you wholeheartedly want to break the addiction from the phone, then this is the stepping stone you've been looking for. After you have suffered without the phone for the better part of 2 days, it's just a matter of being mindful and putting effort in. I know that there are even apps out there now that will lock your phone completely for you, and you get to set the time for how long. Remember to use your airplane mode too!

Your life will open up more, you'll be living life again, to the fullest, and not just going through life.

"And in the end, its not the years in your life that count. Its the life in your years."
-Abraham Lincoln

Average Life Expectancy In the USA is 71 years.

Average time spent using technology a day is 7 hours 20 minutes.

Multiplying that by 365 days equals 2677 hours or 112 days in a year spent interacting with technology.

Multiplying 112 days by 71 years equals 7952 days or 21 years of our lives.

The Average American will roughly spend 21 years of their life engulfed in a virtual world essentially...Wow.

Chapter Two

I Just Like Being Outside

"Death is not the greatest loss in **life**.
The greatest loss is what dies inside us
while we **live**."
- Norman Cousins

I just like being outside. These few words are all I've ever really told people about myself. Behind them though lay so much more meaning. Yes, I like being outside, but in all reality I love being outside. I love adventuring. Love is a strong word, now at 16 years old I know I don't know much about love, but I can honestly say the one thing I love in life is the outdoors.

It's where I feel most at home.

I get more joy from swimming in the ocean or planting a tomato seed or watching the sunset than any one person could know. I'm not the only one who feels this same way, there are many others who have that deep longing: the deep need to be outside. I am not alone, but I'm afraid at the same time that there aren't many of us.

The interesting thing about this "need" I
keep mentioning is that is it's actually in all of us,
but we are losing this beautiful desire to be present
in the natural world. It's in all of us, it's
genetically-wired into us, it's an authentic biological
need that extends back through to our ancestors.

Us and the **earth**, it's the **oldest relationship**
in the world.

A quote comes to mind as I'm writing this,

" Thousands of **tired, nerve-shaken, over civilized people** are beginning to find out going to the mountains is **going home,** the **wilderness is a necessity.** "- John Muir.

I couldn't agree more with Mr. Muir. I've always found that taking the first breath of outside air is one of the sweetest sensations in the world; it's inviting you outside away from all the nonsense and troubles of our daily fabricated life.

Chapter Three

Fact or Fiction

The Leaf Theory

The Leaf Theory? Sounds a little strange, right? You're probably sitting there thinking to yourself, what the hell? Like what drugs is this girl on? Okay, okay, maybe not to that extent, but let me break this down better for you.

Ever walk outside of your front door and the first thing you notice is maybe the sky, the ground that's below your feet, or maybe, simply, a leaf? Just a leaf, could be on a tree, could just be laying still on the ground, or could be blowing about in a gentle breeze. But a leaf is not just a leaf, it is connected to something much greater.

Leaves symbolize and embody life in the natural world.

Clinging to trees, or moving on their own, they remind us of the one single thing in our world that is still pure, still so untouched by our hands, the outdoors.

I created The Leaf Theory when I was about 12 years old. I was out on a walk with my best friend on my road. Mind you, I live in the middle of nowhere so I've got nature engulfing me, but I found myself staring down at the ground, contentedly, watching my feet. Then it hit me, I had been stepping on and crushing some of the most alluring leaves I had seen in my life.

It was Fall and everything was in all its glory before the Winter would come and turn the valleys that I knew so well into nothing but a frosty, winter Arcadia.

There was this one leaf in particular that I can still remember vividly to this day. This leaf was brighter than fire, and yet it had an electric glow around the edges with just a touch of purple where the stem ran through it. It changed the way I look at even the simplest and tinest things in the outdoors.

Whenever I see a leaf it reminds me of that walk, it reminds mc of the clarity that a simple stroll outside can bring to your soul.

I highly recommend The Leaf Theory, go for a walk and you might just be surprised at what comes up or presents itself to you. Whether it be something physical in nature or something symbolic of yourself, you never know. Things come to us at the strangest of times, keep your mind open to the possibilities. Answers can come when we least expect them, even in the outdoors.

> "If we could see the miracle of a single flower clearly, our whole life would change."
> – Buddha

Outdoor Antidote

My cat observation...

Let's turn the wheel a tad and explore my scientific method skills. I am in no sense a scientist or doctor for that matter, but I've always believed in the organic home remedy version of well, everything. It wasn't till about a year after my initial hypothesis of the Leaf Theory that I put pieces together and came up with a full blown "Outdoor Antidote," if you will.

In the summer of 2015 my mom decided it was time to turn our indoor cats(Achilles and Adonis) into outdoor cats.

The day was as perfect as a Pennsylvanian Summer day could get with bright blue skies and smells of something good cooking over a campfire, wafting through the air in my backyard. My mom and I were just sitting out enjoying it all, and one of our 2 cats, whose name is Achilles, was clawing at the patio door. We looked at each other both knowing for awhile now that we had been toying with the idea of transferring the cats outdoors permanently. We had not done it yet because even though we live in a very rural area there are still a few big dogs around us that would just love to play with the cats along with a fairly well-traveled country road in front of our house that for some reason people feel the need to go 90 miles an hour on.

Besides that we knew we had to make them into outdoor cats because they were destroying our house, they had some behavioural problems, and their skin was always scratchy and itchy and attracted fleas, no matter what flea meds we seemed to use. So that afternoon my mom opened up the patio door and let Achilles out.

Let me tell you, the funniest thing happened next, and I'm sitting here writing these very words cracking up just thinking about the situation.

So Achilles walked out with his normal strut (he has an attitude and personality like no cat I've ever met) taking it all in, he was truly enjoying himself. He sauntered over to where my mom was sitting, she was on an outdoor patio lounge chair, and he hopped up with her and that is when he, for lack of a better term, spazzed out.

Yep, you heard me right. My mom and I thought that we had literally just killed Achilles by bringing him outside. His one leg started to lock up and then the other and then he rolled off the chair and kinda did a few sporadic somersaults across the lawn.

(Just envision a New Year's Eve drunk person trying to walk in a straight line.)

We didn't know if we should laugh or cry. Was he having a seizure from being over stimulated by the outdoors? Or what? Was he dying? Did we just kill him? Oh well, within a period of 5 minutes he went from normal to seizure and back to normal. He was fine, kinda like a kid falling off a swing set, they're resilient.

Detox

Ahhh detox. Nowadays we always hear of the word "Detox" but what does it really mean?

To some it's a way of eating and drinking to cleanse the body of toxins, to others it's simply a mindset to break addiction, those are all good but what is an outdoor detox? Ever thought of that?

My hope is that all who read this book will be challenged and inspired that they can take even one simple line out of it and apply it to their life, so how does this relate to detox again? Well I'm focusing more on the detoxing of the smartphones, the television screens, the never ending buzzing of technology that consumes us. Take a step back from it all and detox the wears away from it all.

We didn't know at the time what was happening to him, we still do not exactly know why the sudden episode, but he's been fine since and let me tell you what, every issue we had with both the cats has completely disappeared.

We sit back and laugh at what happened now, but we also realize just how amazing being in a natural habitat could be for them.

Achilles and Adonis had always found someway to pick up fleas even though they were never let outside and had high-level flea meds. Their skin and fur was gross, dusty and dirty always. But within the first month that we had them outside, everything that was sketchy physically had cleared up on them! But how? You would think that they would get worse outside, but it turned out the complete opposite. It was the best decision we ever made as cat owners. The cats are happier and healthier, their fur is beautiful and fuller than it's ever been! They've been thriving as inside and outside cats for almost a year and a half now, and we wouldn't change that decision for the world.

I tend to think of the situation as a huge reflection of our own deep need to be immersed in nature as much as possible. It was amazing to see such a huge transition in the cats, and I've witnessed it on smaller scales in humans.

Nature is the antidote you've been searching for.

The next time you feel sad or depressed, **go outside**. The next time you feel under the weather or just kind of foggy upstairs, **go outside**. The next time you need an answer to your questions, **go outside**. The next time you're feeling frustration or anger, **go outside**.

When you go outside it's like an instant refresh; I can't tell you how many times I solved all my problems by just going outside on a walk. When I head out the door it gives me my peace of mind, the ability to see and think clearly and independently apart from other's opinions, views, and issues.

It's my little antidote that I wanted to share with you all, in hopes that maybe just one person will think about the words I'm writing now and go outside for their own personal well-being.

You can take everything I write and say with a grain of salt, but if you follow this basic procedure of going outside like I do, you won't be disappointed with your outcome.

The Outdoor Antidote I'm referring to will have a MONUMENTAL effect in all aspects of your life.

It's the only therapy I'll ever need, it will also be the only therapy you will need too, if you follow in my steps.

Look at a leaf, or a flower petal, a single blade of grass, let the breeze flow through you, feel the rain or snow touch your skin, let the sun warm you, even kicking a rock as you walk, something! Anything!

To give my body a break, even as I sit here writing this on my computer, I have to take multiple breaks. Being ensconced by it all is deadly.

Chapter Four

Get Out

How Do I Get Outside?

Well, not to be overly simple, but the answer is in the question, get outside.

I have people ask me all the time what they should be doing when they're outside or how to get outside more. Never in my life did I ever have to ask such questions, but I'm learning and realizing that getting outside is a huge ordeal for some people. So again, "How do I get Outside?" Well, go to any door in your house… Sorry, I'm getting sarcastic, but all in all it's just about making that mental decision that, yes, I'm going outside. It can be as simple as taking a walk to being as complex as "I'm going to backpack the Appalachian Trail."

Everyone starts somewhere; some start from birth, others start a little later in life or not at all, the matter of the fact is is that the outdoors are for everyone.

No tree is going to say, "Get off my trail!" just like no ocean will spit you back out and tell you to go back to your smartphone. It's the most welcoming place because it's our true home, for everyone. Once you spend a night under the stars or take a dip in a cool lake, you're hooked; it's real, it's real emotions, and it's real physical sensations.

Final thought on this topic is it shouldn't ever be a huge deal, take a walk breathing in that good air, plant a seed for a new day and open your eyes to the single most amazing thing, the outdoors.

Taken at Folly Beach, South Carolina, USA.

Chapter Five

The Dying Breed

Long gone are the pioneers, the adventurers, the free spirits, and those with wild hearts. My last statement isn't entirely true, but truth lies within it. We have not lost our need to be outside but it is being strangled and hidden deep inside us because we care more about what's trending on Twitter, rather than looking for new places outside to explore.

Don't be the one who lets the need for adventure and the outdoors die inside you. Everyone, and I mean EVERYONE is here on this planet for a reason, and everyone has a need for wanderlust. It is a part of us, the outdoors, there is no denying it. You just have to be the one to choose if you will carry on with adventuring out into this world; don't be a part of the dying breed, be a pioneer, be an adventurer, be a free spirit, and have a wild heart for all days to come.

Squelched At Birth

F ar too often nowadays I have observed parents as a contributing factor to raising and ruining our modern generation's epigenetics.

I am a lucky one.

I was technically born in the suburban areas surrounding Washington, DC, but I moved to Northwest Pennsylvania at the age of two. So I've always counted myself as a country girl in a sense, no not a cowgirl, but definitely a girl of the natural world.

I grew up alongside my best friend Emily. We have lived within twenty feet of each other practically my whole life. Again I will say it, I am a lucky one, Em is a lucky one too.

So why were we so lucky?

We were not raised in front of a screen. A rare thing in recent decades.

We played outside from dawn until dusk. Hours and hours we would spend outside, any season, it did not matter. It could be 13 degrees outside, in the dead of January, and we'd be out making snow mounds and tunnels with not a care in the world. We'd come inside completely frozen, but with the biggest smiles in the world on our faces.

Even when I was at my Dad's house every other weekend in the summer when I was younger we'd get outside. Which wasn't really his thing, but he knew my sister, Ari and I loved it so much so he ventured out anyway.

He lived close to Presque Isle State Park, right on Lake Erie. We would head over to Beach One and just beachcomb for hours. (Beachcombing is a more appropriate term for scouring a shoreline for beach glass, shells, and other random treasures that have washed ashore) Jumping in and out of the water, maybe finding a shell that wasn't actually smashed to pieces, it was great! Moments I'll never forget, and that I will cherish for years to come. My time was cut short with my Dad, but it doesn't change the fact he still made that effort to get us outside, Thank you, Dad.

That's all it is, an effort, a choice made by yourself to get you and those around you outside and really living life how it should be lived.

Anyways, I remember in particular during the summers of our youth, Em and I would venture out far. Barefooted and equipped with blankets and whatever else we could dig up between our garages, we'd head out into the fields that surround our houses and then into the woods to make forts using fallen branches and sticks. We walk back there every now and then and can find the remnants of our forts, with a blanket in one still!

We would eat green beans from her garden and then go eat blueberries from the bushes in my yard. This was the usual during those long summer days.

I remember one summer in particular; Em and I kinda adopted a large pine tree that's located right in between our houses. We cleared out all the small twigs and sticks and made a perfect climbing path up this giant tree. Now when I mean big, I'm meaning big, this tree is huge, I am talking Rockefeller Center Christmas tree big. At about the 40 foot mark we made a fort, and we'd spend all day, yes, ALL DAY up in this tree. We hauled so much random junk up and down this tree, umbrellas, two by fours, shovels, house siding, pieces of a ladder, and even lawn chairs. (dead serious...there is still a license plate hanging up in this tree to this day) It was epic.

There was another summer I distinctly reminisce about, Em and I were going into fourth and fifth grade at the time. I had this camper that we ended up bringing home and putting in the backyard. It was rough simply due to having not been used in awhile, so Em and I naturally made it our mission to clean it up and live in it for the summer. We did too. Of course we didn't spend every night in it, but we sure did spend plenty of nights out there just hanging out. We'd stay out by my fire pit till around 11 on a weeknight and on weekends we sometimes didn't sleep.

We would just watch the fire and the stars till the sun came up. There was this one time where a stray dog was out wandering around our fire and he just adopted us for the the night, so we being us decided to let the dog stay in the camper to with us that night. He left in the morning just as quickly as he came. I'll still always remember that night as clear as day. Good times, that I will tell about for the rest of my life.

As Em and I got older we saw wider ranges for us to explore, my sister also started driving so that was a huge plus. We really started hiking in our local state park. There are awesome overlooks, waterfalls, and just a lot of history around us, so needless to say we explore it all. We also have a friend named Griffin who started to join us on hikes in middle school and still to this day we are always adventuring.

There was this one hike in particular that included Emily, Griffin, I, and another friend of ours named Ryan. We were about sixth and seventh grade if I'm remembering right.

So we started out at Emily's house, just hanging in her driveway till everyone got there. We ventured out through her driveway and up our road to get to the trail. Past my house, the cemetery, the horses and dogs at almost the end of the road, and onward to the farm we walked. Once we got to the farm from there we could cut down onto the trail, we visited with the owners of the farm of course too. We all knew each other, and our families had known each other for many years back; grandparents and back. (My grandpa had actually wrestled and played football with the owner of the farm when they were in High School together, and still stayed friends for many years). So we cut down through their cow field and right at the base of that field on the other side of the fence was the trail.

Emerging through the wires in the fence we stumbled onto the trail together. The trail we were on is called the Gerard Hiking Trail located in Oil Creek State Park. This section of the trail that we came out on is actually at an overlook in the park, so we all wandered over to take in the view. It overlooks a beautiful old wooden bridge called Miller Farm bridge, it lays across Oil Creek and is surrounded by the valley.

That bridge was actually our destination that day, so we wandered on down the trail that would lead us to the bridge. We all knew the way, most of us grew up hiking these trails with our parents, it was second nature to us. Down the switchbacks we went, swinging on random old grape vines we found. At the bottom of "Switchback Mountain" as we call it is the bike trail. Taking a left onto that we continued through a small hidden deer path and onto the road that leads to the bridge.

We basically hiked in one big "C" shape, the overlook is directly across from the bridge. It's pretty cool looking and thinking about it, about how a half hour ago we had been at the overlook looking at the bridge and now we are on the bridge looking up at the overlook.

We dropped down from the bridge and underneath to the creek. We spent a solid two hours swimming, catching crayfish, attempting to catch some bluegill (no such luck). But we did have plenty of luck catching crayfish… like lobster sized ones. So somewhere along the lines we got this brilliant idea to cook some of the crayfish we had caught.

You sure bet we cooked them too.

We managed to find an old can under the bridge, Ryan and Griffin had lighters, Emily had a half filled water bottle, all we had to do was find some sticks and we were set.

Griffin got to work making a small fire pit over a large bowl shaped river rock. Emily, Ryan, and I set to work on gathering the twigs and small sticks. We got the fire going, CONTAINED and thriving. Placed the can in with the water and started boiling our crayfish. It worked, it worked quite well, if I do say so. We all had a bite, and none of us died, golly gee what a concept. We squelched the fire and decided to bring the can back with us. We went on our merry ways back up across the bridge, over the bike trail, scaled Switchback Mountain again, crawled through the old barbed fence, through the cow field, waved goodbye to the farm owners, walked back down our road past the horses and dogs, the cemetery, and then the few neighboring houses to our own driveways.

I'll be sharing that story for a long long long time.

Currently Griff, Em, I, and a few others have got a plan to stay in the local adirondack shelters, probably over Christmas break is what we are aiming for right now.

This is a picture I captured in November of 2015 while camping at the adirondacks. Pretty stoked to get back during this winter for a night in them, of course surrounded by my friends who share the same appreciation for them. (Don't worry! They get pretty toasty even in zero degrees)

Helicopter Parenting and the Damage it has Done

I want to stress this, I am lucky. I am beyond grateful and thankful to the people who raised me and influenced me from such a young age, the ones who gave me freedom to explore my natural surroundings. Who let me make my own choices and decisions when out and about. Did I fall and get hurt ever? Hell yeah I did, but I learned how to fall, adapt, grow, move, think, learn, and respect the habitat around me. I wouldn't have wanted it any other way. My inner primalness wasn't squelched and condensed into modern society's small box, that is labeled how parents should raise their kids.

A majority of parents today just suck.

Yep, I just said that. No, I will never take it back either. I've seen one too many times just how bad modern parenting has screwed kids up. My only question is how?

How did you all manage to be raised so freely and yet you keep your kids on such a short leash?

I remember having it drilled into my head in school sessions regarding "stranger danger," and "don't take candy from random strangers." Well you know what, I wasn't one to talk to strange beings because I had enough sense and clarity not to, and I didn't like candy… we don't give kids enough credit. I didn't need a week long lecture every school year from first grade on. But still as I got older everything transitioned more from worrying about strangers in random cars on the street to the ones trying to connect and hack you online. We've all heard those stories of how online predators befriend kids online and then they agree to meet in person. Yes those are scary, and, yes, those situations shouldn't be taken lightly, but many could have been avoided.

Kids get sneaky. In many of those online situations the kids were simply trying to avoid parents that hovered over them **all the time**. So they'd open up to random creepers who seriously did have bad intentions just because a parent(s) was constantly in control and making every single decision for their kid.

When a parent becomes too overprotective and controlling, the kid loses the ability to think for themselves, rationally if I might add. So all of a sudden when the internet became more accessible to kids in the 2000's nothing was threatening really. Everything was happy go lucky and it was so easy for people to get caught up talking to randoms online in early chat rooms. Of course kids loved it, they could meet and befriend people from literally all over the world. But you see up until this point in their lives a parent had made every decision for them. So naturally they couldn't decipher a predator from just another kid like themselves.

This is just one instance where helicopter parents have royally screwed up. I have dozens upon dozens of situations we could revisit and analyze, but I might as well just start on another book for that.

Okay, so I probably just insulted many people, and I didn't even touch on how to fix this dilemma. Let us begin.

We have established this modern epidemic of over-parenting. So the question is now:

How do we un-parent?

Un-parenting and Reconnecting

Simplest thing I can say about un-parenting is for the parent(s) to shut their own mouth for two seconds, listen to their kid, like REALLY listen for once, and realize that their kid is a person of this world, living just like the rest of us.

We must stop making every decision for our kids, and instead provide guidance when guidance is needed.

The power of play and a kid's own well-being directly correlate to one another.

We desensitize our kids. We aren't teaching them to swim and ride bikes anymore. I see parents stick their kids in front of a T.V. and call it good. I lifeguarded at my local pool this summer and observed parents just sticking their kids in a lifevest and think that that is okay. Swimming is a basic essential skill that EVERYONE should have and utilize whether it be for play or survival, period.

Better yet, when I see parents hand their kids their smartphones and the kids will sit in the same position, eyes locked to that tiny screen, playing games for hours. The parents do it so that the kid's won't bother them, and so that the parents can selfishly continue to do their own thing while their kid is "entertained." Numbed is the better word. And, that's dehumanizing.

It is unnatural.

The best person I've ever had explain this epidemic to me was Richard Louv, author of the book *Last Child in the Woods.* I haven't personally had a conversation with him yet, I've only read his works. I do not know if there's anyone out there who grasps this topic as Louv does. He recognizes the severity of modern parenting and the effects it's having on our children.

He explains flawlessly the importance of informal natural play.

"A magnificent case for unplugging our kids from the Net and letting them roam free again in the woods." - Mike Davis on Louv's book *Last Child in the Woods*.

I've always kinda felt like the last child in the woods.

Yes, there are plenty others still like me, and I'd like to think there is a definite resurgence in kids reconnecting with the outdoors and just playing.

I recently read an article about a man by the name of Mike Lanza. He gets it, no helicopter parenting on his part. He resides in high-tech Silicon Valley but what he has done for his kids is simply amazing. He turned his suburban backyard into a free range, creativity cultivating, child play area.

"Kids have to find their own balance of power."
- Mike Lanza

His kids and the neighboring kids are free to play and roam as they please. How it should be.

I've deeply stressed reconnection but the thing is, we would not need to be reconnected if we weren't ever unconnected in the first place.

So we must start at the beginning, and make sure disconnection from the outdoors never takes place. We must start with our kids.

Chapter Six

Wonders and Worries

I Want to Do That Too...

And you can.

Have you seen an outdoor activity that really sparked your interest? Kayaking maybe? Snowboarding? Spear Fishing? There is SO much to be doing outside. Something at one time has caught your attention I bet, and if you don't at least try it now, you'll be kicking yourself later that you didn't. I've found that my passions have lead me to activities such as windsurfing, paddleboarding, sustainable gardening, trail running, snowboarding, longboarding, backpacking/camping, kayaking, kiteboarding, among many other activities; I don't sit for very long, if you haven't noticed.

The best part is once you start learning and broadening your horizons in the outdoor recreation world, you won't stop.

I'm constantly trying to learn new things, like the ones I've listed above. These outdoor activities grow with you, you'll never stop improving and learning; we should never stop learning. I still have things on my list that I want to do in life, and eventually I will, now it's your turn to get interested in what outdoor activities you want to do. You've got a life to live, you've got a body and a mind that can do so much, put your aspirations into motion.

Remember, " A ship in harbour is safe. But that's not what ships are built for."
                                              - William Shedd.

How do I start though? If you see something you wanna do, go learn and educate yourself on everything there is to know about that activity. This is a good time to utilize modern technology, use it to your advantage for research, there are hundreds of articles and videos specializing in outdoor activities. Figure out what you're going to need for it, do you need an instructor? Or a guide maybe? What gear may you need for it, if any?

Say, for example, if you're really interested in snowboarding, you'll have to figure where the nearest ski slopes are. You'll probably want to rent the equipment (board w/ bindings and boots, usually available at the resorts) the first few times till you are really hooked, which you will be. Lastly you'll want to look into lessons, a good instructor will get you up and going much faster than if you tried to learn on your own. Learn the lingo and the culture, all that comes with the activity. (Maybe you have a friend who snowboards, most people are more than willing to share something they love with anyone.)

"Learn something new, try something different, convince yourself you have no limits". -Brian Tracy.

You won't be disappointed when you get to enjoy whatever activity(s) you choose to do for the rest of your life. The people you'll meet, the friends you'll share it all with, the memories you'll make, now that's living life.

"*Somebody should tell us, right at the start of our lives, that we are dying. Then we might live life to the limit, every minute of every day. Do it! I say. Whatever you want to do, do it now! There are only so many tomorrows*" - Pope Paul IV

Right on Pope Paul IV!

Right on!

Best Zoo in the World

One of the best parts of getting outside is also encountering/ observing animals in their natural habit. Some of my best memories while out and about in the natural world come from stumbling across wildlife. Seeing dolphins swim alongside the ferry boat I was on, watching a bald eagle fly overhead while I was kayaking near twilight, viewing white tailed deer playing in a field when I was on a day hike, and best yet catching a glimpse of manta rays gliding along underneath my board

when I was windsurfing once. Those memories are forever in my brain, and for that I'm grateful.

Of course, with anything you have to be careful, but it also shouldn't scare you from enjoying life and the outdoors too. I remember back one time when my mom was trail running she... well... she basically body slammed a black bear. She was unharmed thankfully, and she probably had never ran so fast in her life, but it'll also never stop her from being out in the places she loves most, and it shouldn't. My mom is also an extremely special case, if there is a bear around they'll cross paths at least once, guaranteed. But I'm completely the opposite I always hope I'll see a bear and I never do, oh well. There was one once, a black bear named Kevin who lived in a campground I was at for the weekend. No need to worry though, Kevin was more like a puppy then a bear, but you also never know with wild animals so it never hurts to stay cautious.

One of the best ways to stay safe when dealing with wildlife is to just stay aware.

As long as you are paying attention to what's going on around you, you mostly won't have to deal with any issues. Just learn to look for animal prints, droppings, and if you're at the ocean just be prepared to deal with the aquatic wildlife that comes with that environment, among other signs which tell you that animals are near and just stay alert (varies depending on which climate and habitat you're in) . Remember nothing out there is intentionally going to make a beeline for you, go out and enjoy the outdoor activity you came to do, and you'll probably get the chance to view some pretty amazing animals while you are at it.

Staying Safe

I am by no means a safety stickler, but between my background in lifeguarding and just outdoor experience in general, it never hurts to pass a few tips along. One thing is to always have a partner or group with you, and if you're going at it alone, let someone know where you are going and around what time you are planning to be back. My mom trail runs alone a lot, so she'll always let me know what her game plan is. You just never know what could happen, so it's a precaution to take to cover your back just in case.

Another thing, of course, is to just be aware of the wildlife in whatever area you are currently enjoying. Most importantly is to always be prepared, gear wise, first aid, be prepared for weather, situations can change fast so just be prepared. Keep your head clear and focus on the task the may be presented to you, and if you can follow those two things, it'll keep you and others a lot safer than those who don't.

Chapter Seven

Whole New View

A Change in Heart

Maybe, just maybe, my words have swayed you, or not. But if you are starting to have *a change in heart*, and are truly wanting to change your life, for a more outdoorsy lifestyle, I want to congratulate you. If you're seriously interested in setting down your phone and picking up the trekking poles you have made a life choice that will only ever benefit you, I'm so stoked for you!

By investing yourself in the great outdoors, you have already begun changing your mindset, which will give you a clear head but this is a great thing simply for your body, your health.

Body, mind, and the outdoors are all connected, you'll thank yourself later, I'm sure.

I want to connect with everyone, young or old, female or male, families or solo, the outdoors are for everyone to enjoy. May we start a revolution of adventurers together.

Greater Appreciation

The most humbling experiences in my life have mostly come from my outdoor excursions. I now have the deepest appreciation for our planet, it has given so much to me, so whenever I can I try to give back. I'm not extreme by any means, but a little bit here and a little bit there will always help, especially if more people become mindful of their practices. I've been composting for some time now, I'll recycle, and reuse when I can. I'll pick up trash when I see it, and I refuse to use disposable plastic bottles. For example, even though we are on our own well, we prefer to collect wild spring water and fill our own reusable water bottles, rather than buying corporate/store-packaged water and adding more plastic to the already overflowing landfills.

As I said, a little bit here and a little bit there can help, and for this gorgeous world we all live in, it's worth me taking the time out of my day to think and act upon it.

Confidence.

Confidence comes from within.

How does confidence and the outdoors correlate?

The truth of the matter is, that the outdoors has this funny way of throwing itself all at you sometimes. Whether it be the road you're taking or the stream you're swimming in, nature always finds a way to throw some curve balls

It wasn't too long ago that I was out on a trail run with my mom when in our path lay an 80 foot tree spread all over the path. It completely decimated the trail, no sight of where the path lay beyond, all there was, was tree, and a lot of it. So just as naturally as that tree had fallen, my mom and I began to meander and climb our way through it, in hopes of finding the other side. We traveled left among the tree's branches for awhile with no such luck of finding our trail again. We clambered back through to the right this time, moving forward and what do you know we spotted the path finally after about 25 minutes of legitimate searching. Crawling out of the tree's grip and into some pricker bushes, but lucky for us the path lay just a few feet ahead.

Our half hour trail run may have turned into an hour long trail run, but no biggy, honestly. In fact I wouldn't have wanted it any other way, I shared plenty of good laughs with my mom, got some solid scrapes and bruises to tell a good story, and I learned and grew from that experience. You never know what could come at you, and that's in all aspects of life.

You problem solve, come up with a solution, act on it, and then are better prepared for the next time. You have a problem and conquer it, that's what builds confidence. Confidence that you can take with you for the next time around, because if we are all being truthful, life never lets you get too comfortable for long. That is not a bad thing, either. Yes, I agree that in some people confidence has come naturally to them, but in others not so much. It can definitely be a building process for most, so get outside and start building it. Build it through climbing over rocks and trees and roots, crossing rivers and swimming against the current. You'll thank yourself later.

You've Got Options

Oh the options... more then I can count on all ten fingers. You've got them, now you just have to do a little exploring for yourself.

There are so many ways to get outside, as I've said, but I figured I'd take the time to somewhat categorize it all, best I can.

Camping / Hiking / Backpacking, all of which can be done anywhere at anytime of the year with the right gear. You never know how much fun you can have until you start chucking pine cones at your sister. But, on a serious note, the beauty of all three, the camping, the hiking, and the backpacking is that all offer something different. You can take a simple walk in the woods, or you could take it a step further and carry all you need to sustain yourself on your back while taking a walk.

With camping you can make it as remote or as modern as you'd like, it still gets you out there. With a simple bivy bag, to a hammock, to a tent, to a camper, to an R.V., it all gets you out there. Or just take a walk. Whenever I have a friend who wants to hang out I always take them on a hike, we can talk forever and still enjoy all that the outdoors have to offer. My family and I camp A LOT and we backpack A LOT, and usually with friends most of the time. It's great, really I'm not leading you all astray, I promise, It's fun!

Hunting / Fishing to get real primal. Honestly, catching your first fish is one of the greatest feelings. I was probably 5 or 6 fishing with my Grandpa, and I caught a Bluegill, and you bet I gutted that fish, cooked it over the fire, and I ate it (pretty sure I didn't even share any of it!). No way was I going to waste good meat (I would never make it as a Vegetarian or Vegan). With hunting, well, humans have been doing it since the beginning to survive, and I'd much rather eat something I processed myself than a piece of meat processed in God knows where/ when, covered in preservatives, wrapped in plastic…
* cringes*.

Water Sports… the broadest group and my favorite. I've been growing up in the water, it's second nature to me. I've been swimming in lakes, rivers, and oceans all my life. I would tandem kayak with my mom when I was really little, and then at around 7, I progressed to my own kayak. At 8 I started Windsurfing and at 12 I started teaching alongside my mom's fiance, Mike (I've probably taught close to 150 people by now). I joined the swim team in 7th grade and right around that time we invested in paddleboards. I took up surfing about 2 years ago, and I'm still learning and always will be, but I LOVE it!

At the beginning of last school year I took a semester long Red Cross Lifeguarding course through my school and got certified. This past Summer I lifeguarded during the season at my local pool, and I continue to lifeguard at my local school's pool throughout the year. The most recent watersport that I've been wanting to try for a long time is Kiteboarding, so in July I got connected in with an amazing teacher, and I can honestly say I'm so excited to be increasing my skill in Kiting. All of these just kinda skim the top of the water sport world, but it just begins to show all that the water has to offer.

Biking is simply great; there's road biking, rail trails, mountain biking (my favorite), BMX, and just a great casual way of transportation or spending time with the family. You'll also get a pretty great workout from any of it, all while spending time outdoors.

Running is definitely the most accessible and fastest way to get outdoors and active. You technically don't even need shoes, I love barefooting it when I can!

We as humans have been running for ages, there's no equipment, it's just you against yourself, but it's fun too.

Running is in my blood; my mom ran both cross country and track in high school, so, of course, I chose to run both cross country and track, Both are great sports, if I do say so myself. The only difference between my mom and myself is in track, she ran hurdles, and I sprint with some middle distance mixed in on occasion. In recent years my mom took up trail running, or ultra running as some call it; basically it's endurance running just on trails. Cross country on steroids, as I like to call it. What a rush, if I could just trail run over regular running, I would. You never get bored because your surroundings are always changing on you, it's awesome! The big plus to running is you're also getting the workout of a lifetime from it, it's a win win.

Photography covers more of the leave no trace type of lifestyle. Taking pictures leaves you with an entire collection of memories that you can look back on and show to friends and family. Take pictures of the sunrise and sunset, the trees, the ocean, a valley, a lake, a mountain range, your feet, and all the animals you come across.

Photo of me, taking photos at a local mountain bike race. Thanks Mike!

I was lucky enough to have an amazing photographer come into my life and show me the ways of the lens...even if I don't quite utilize this power all the time. Forever thankful for Michael, the best photographer I know. Throughout the years with him I know my view of the world has been shaped by him and his vision as a top-notch photographer.

Winter Sports is also a very broad category. I snowboard, but I also learned how to downhill ski too, it just happened that I connected more with snowboarding over skiing (it's a more natural motion to me since board sports are kinda my thing). I also have the great opportunity to be a snowboarding instructor, can't wait for that! But I do also love to cross-country ski, and boy I'll tell you what, it is one of the BEST workouts you can get and it's super fun, which is always a plus.

It'll be 16 degrees out at night in the Winter and my mom and I will head over to the local cross country trails, and we'll go out in just lined leggings, an Under Armour shirt, and with light gloves on because you work up that much of a sweat. It's kinda unreal to be going out in the dead of winter trucking along out in the moonlight woods, you'll see the moon sparkling off the snow crystals, and it's so super bright out there that even the trees have shadows, it's unreal.

Anyways, there are plenty of other activities to partake in; polar plunging, ice skating, hockey, ice fishing, snowshoeing, sledding, and this coming winter I'll be taking up ice kiting! So much to do!

A daily harvest.

Gardening makes you one with nature; you are literally aiding in the natural process of plant growth. I definitely believe we as humans benefit greatly from gardening. I used to garden along with my grandpa, and eventually I took over.

In recent years I started using wooden pallets for my garden, I've grown tomatoes, corn, string beans, peppers, cabbage, broccoli, cauliflower, among many other things. On my family's property we also have an apple orchard, two peach trees, tons of blueberry bushes, grape vines, and a raspberry patch. We used to have a plum tree too, unfortunately it caught a blight and we had to chop it down.

Back to my original point though, we gain so much from gardening, it gets us outside, and we harvest beautiful fruits and veggies that we know aren't covered in waxes, pesticides, and picked before ripe to deliver it over 2,000 miles to rot in a grocery store of your choosing. This year we hosted four beehives to help pollinate our orchards and gardens. We were shocked at the bumper crops we harvested this year because of the bees. So, embrace your green thumb and get growing.

Alfred Austin once said, " The glory of gardening hands in the dirt, head in the sun, heart with nature. To nurture a garden is to feed not just the body, but the soul.".

Other random things that don't really fit into a specific category, but I wanted to mention: Rock climbing, longboarding skateboarding, rollerblading, martial arts (rooted outside in the elements), yoga, kite flying, horseback riding, ropes courses, zip-lining, catching lightning bugs even! This list doesn't even come close to all that's out there to enjoy in the realm of Outdoor Recreation, so just pick something and start!

Chapter Eight

Brighter Horizons

Adventure

Be an *adventurer*.

So far I've talked mostly of just being outside, and getting outdoors, and the more technical side of it all, but now I really want to focus in on Adventure. Now the actual definition of the word "Adventure" refers to an experience, and what I'm trying to pull out of that is we should be creating experiences, or adventures!

Everything in life is an experience, but not everything is an adventure.

Some people speak of the adventures they want to have, they make a bucket list of all the places they want to go. That is great! But all too often I see people talk more than they do. Don't be that person who talks of the wild adventures they will have and then never acts on it. You, and only you, are the sole proprietor of what you will do and be. Go be the adventurer in this world of ordinary beings.

71

Eating, seeing, breathing are all experiences for the senses, but how about giving the senses an adventure? Eating a wild edible (with an expert, of course) during peak season, seeing the sunrise over a valley filled with fog at dawn, all the different colors in the sky and the subtle changes that happen in just a few short minutes, or breathing in wild ocean air. That all comes with adventure, which is found in stepping outdoors.

Two books that mainly shaped the way I think of adventure are *The Way of Adventure* by Jeff Salz. PH. D. and *Microadventures* by Alastair Humphreys. Both AMAZING books and guys, they just grasp what life is really about, yet both have their own unique way of viewing the world. In the book *The Way of Adventure* Dr. Jeff Salz talks deeply about the need for adventure in our lives, he also shares some of his adventures, which are pretty amazing. On the other hand there is Alastair Humphreys; one of the greatest things about Alastair is his knack for showing people just how simple getting outside can be, and making it an adventure too. In his book *Microadventures* he shares the wonder of just taking a swim in a river to building a wild hut (which, if I do say so myself, is quite fun). I'd recommend both reads to anyone, but especially to you all that chose to read this very book.

"The greatest adventure is what lies ahead "
- J.R.R Tolkien (my favorite author)

Long Live the Story Tellers

I love listening to stories that my mom shares with me about when she grew up, all of their camping trips, all the adventures that came with them. My mom's fiance, Mike, also tells me of all his amazing adventures alongside his dad, their trips out west and camping every Summer at the seashore. Simply awesome stories and memories.

Then I thought to myself, what will my generation be telling their kids and grandkids?

Something along the lines of, I remember when I got my first iPhone or something similar. Makes for a great story, huh? No, it does not, not even a little.

But I'll get to be the one who tells of the time I slept in a hammock and woke up with frost on my sleeping bag, and how I had the most incredible view, overlooking a foggy lake with the sun rising over a hillside. Or of the times spent backpacking with my family and some of our friends, just unforgettable experiences all the way around. The best part is that they were all spent in the outdoors, away from the screens, nothing compares.

73

Storytelling is becoming a lost art form, not because there isn't still plenty of stories out there, but because we aren't creating new ones of worth. I'm lucky that I'm growing up in and around people that'll share their adventures with me. They inspired me to create adventures of my own and now I can share some of my stories with all of you.

I remember back to my first trip to the ocean. My family and I went to the Cape Hatteras National Seashore in North Carolina. From the moment I got there and till this very day it's still my favorite place in the world, as of right now (always subject to change in the future, as I still plan on seeing many places new to me). I'm very much a water person and the beauty of this place is that you have the ocean on one side and the Pamlico Sound on the other, both incredible bodies of water. This place is like no other, it's more secluded, I forgot to mention that it's also a barrier island, and at its furthest part away from the mainland it is about 50 miles of just the Pamlico Sound. It's where I first learned how to windsurf, kiteboard, and so much more. We like to go Ghost crab hunting, which is one of the most entertaining things, honestly by the time we are done my sides hurt from laughing so long. I've also met some pretty amazing people down there; unforgettable days, with unforgettable people. I'll be telling stories of my times spent there for the rest of my life, truly unforgettable stories. Plenty more still to come.

The best stories seem to all have the same common theme, they are all outside. Around a fire, on top of a mountain, or floating down a river, with friends and family. Good stories can come from solo trips too, but sharing the experience with others sure adds some different color to it.

A wise person once said, "Collect moments not things."

Get outside and go make stories of your own, ones that your grandkids will tell their grandkids and so on, good stories never die.

Oh, the Places You'll Go

I preach to you all that getting outside is simply taking that step out your front door and it truly is! But eventually you'll get to a point where you branch out and seek out different destinations to explore and try new things. So this brings us to traveling; I'm far from being a world traveler, but of some of the places I have gone, I have taken back with me memorable adventures of all sorts. From exploring Sedona in Arizona, to the quaint beaches

I cherish along the east coast, to Mackinac Island of Michigan, the mountains surrounding Denver, Colorado and so on. One of my favorite backpacking trips took place about 3 hours southeast from where I live currently. Yet I still have so many more places to explore, more countries to be stamped onto my passport, more thrilling adventures to be had, and to see jaw-dropping sights all around this planet.

" The world is a book and those who do not travel only read one page"
                                              - St. Augustine.

Life Long Friendships and Unbreakable Bonds

In a world that contains a total of 7.4 billion people, you are bound to meet some characters out there.

Some of the most fascinating conversations I've had occured while I was outside. Everyone has something to share, so always listen, exchange smiles with strangers, and remember kindness is contagious. There's just something so freeing about talking with another person while enjoying the outdoors. I've got friends from all over, and yet the furthest ones away I met through surfing or snowboarding, for example (my luck). But it's all good, once you spend some time out in nature with others, you create a pretty strong bond.

Nature is funny in that sense, it has a way of always bringing people together, which in our modern crazy times is something that is much needed by everyone.

"How far we travel in life matters far less than those we meet along the way."
- Robert Louis Stevenson

Document Your Adventures

I hope that you'll eventually get to a point where you want to capture your adventures. Again, this is the time to take advantage of modern technology, grab the phone camera, or even reach for the latest action sports camera (I'm fairly fond of my Gopro Hero 3... just saying) and share all your adventures with your friends and family, make them want to join you the next time!

Show them what they are missing out on!

It's also a neat idea to keep an adventure journal with you. Write down all you did, what you saw, smelled, touched, and tasted throughout the journey. You could even draw pictures or write a poem about what you experienced during your adventures. By documenting your adventures it's also an awesome way of keeping the stories you created alive, just like I mentioned earlier.

Chapter Nine

A 16 Year Old and The Natural World

So Why Should I Listen to a 16 Year Old Girl?

Yes, I'm 16, yes I'm a girl, has that made you question things? Like why is it even relevent to listen and take my information seriously?

Well you can take it or leave it, anything I say. Most of what I've observed between the human connection to the outdoors is from personal experience, but not completely. Plenty was bred into me, but also I've done a lot of my own personal research. I'm always reading and asking questions, which leads me to more reading. A person also naturally uses the scientific process when exploring and discovering. It's natural problem solving.

The book *Last Child in the Woods* by Richard Louv is absolutely, 100%, a book that everyone should read.

"The children and nature movement is fueled by this fundamental idea: the child in nature is an endangered species, and the health of children and the health of the Earth are inseparable."

- Richard Louv.

He just gets it, every aspect of it all; the big picture. One of my favorite parts of the book comes from part 2 *Why the Young (and the Rest of Us) Need Nature*, Louv talks about a woman by the name of Elaine Brooks. Brooks says, "Once our ancestors climbed high in that tree, there was something about looking out over the land - something that healed us quickly." (pg. 42 Ch. 4). It's so pure, the entire book, hard truth.

One more book I'd like to mention is *Go Wild* by John J. Ratey, MD and Richard Manning. Both men seamlessly explain the link between us and the outdoors and why we need it to survive. The moment you start reading is the moment you start learning and retraining your brain on all you think you know about modern life. *Go Wild* gets deep into the nitty gritty of our past and where we all came from and what we should be holding onto. If you are a person who needs "facts" to prove why you should be outdoors more, READ *Go Wild* right now.

A Little Piece of Heaven

I'm not religious in any sense really. I have a much more deistic view of the world, but there is no denying that what we have here on our earth is special, all around us it is heavenly.

"Every flower of the field, every fiber of a plant, every particle of an insect, carries with it the impress of its Maker, and can - if duly considered - read us lectures of ethics or Divinity."
- Thomas Blount

We live in a nirvana, we really really do. It surrounds us, it consumes us in the best way possible, only if you let it.

We go inside to pray yet the only times I've ever felt a true spiritual presence was when I was kneeling in the grass, sand, mud, or water. It's in those moments you realize and can feel that we did not come into this world by chance.

You are not just cosmic matter left over from a cataclysmic reunion of galactic matter.

The outdoors is alive, in every sense of the word alive. It breathes, and sees, and it heals, giving off vibes and radiating positive energy.

It's just like when an amazing person comes into your life. Their vibe and presence makes you see in a different light. You strive to be a greater person yourself because of this individual, kinda like when you really except nature into your life too.

The universe, the great outdoors, mother earth if you want, when let in, opens your eyes to more than you and I know. It is different for each person, that awakening within.

It can be a subtle shake inside or a lion roaring, just waiting to get out and explore.

"NO LONGER CONSCIOUS OF MY MOVEMENT, I DISCOVERED A NEW UNITY WITH NATURE. I HAD FOUND A NEW SOURCE OF POWER AND BEAUTY, A SOURCE I NEVER DREAMT EXISTED." **- Roger Bannister**

Chapter 10

Bringing All The Elements Together

There is something magnificently different in the chemical makeup of a human being when immersed in the natural world.

"These mountains that you are carrying, you were only supposed to climb."
-Najwa Zebian

The massive tidal wave of technology was thrust upon us as humans who were once so deeply-connected to the natural seasons, cycles, and creatures, yet we know not yet the damage it has done and will do to us as a species. Forever drowning in a sea of unknowing consequences.

Our modern culture has been sculpted to perform in an artificial environment, yet we do not know how to live in a real one. Every ounce of our essence is teeming with synthetic matter, when in all reality we should be filled with our world's organic matter. We wish for peace of mind, but yet find shelter in closed off places.

How would one ever obtain an open, clear mind when shut in a box?

They wouldn't.

Only those who open up. Open up every part of themselves to the world around them.

Again, embrace.

Embrace your primal side, utilize it, transform the energy gained from it; create more, do more, play more, inspire, re-energize, empower.

In every aspect of the words **Primal Reconnection** there lies truth, clarity, peace, mindfulness, completeness, natural enlightenment. The list goes on...

Life is challenging.

There is no denying that.

But why make it any more challenging than it needs to be by losing yourself in the virtual world?

I do not discredit technology in the sense that I don't appreciate the good sides to it all. I've had the apps, still do in some cases. I've been using google docs to write this very book on my home computer and sometimes a laptop. I call and I text just like everyone else does. I've been sucked into the vortex that is social media in some cases. I am human.

But I also do not let it run my life.

I am fueled by the naturalist form of energy in the world. Because it is the world that I am fueled by.

We as humans should always be evolving and creating, but there are fine lines when one starts to drift to far into a world with nothing but man-made elements. Out of touch with real elements, true reality.

I can only ask of you to absorb what I have said throughout this book. Take it or leave it. I mean I would totally love it and be stoked out of my mind if you did apply these words to your own life, that is my ending goal always.

I must keep reminding myself that even the smallest rock, when tossed into the water, will create ripples.

With love,
Tasha Sabatini

Check out more of my works! On tashasabatini.com

Subscribe to my YouTube channel at
YouTube/Tasha Sabatini

Join me on Facebook at Tasha Sabatini!

See me and get to know me on Instagram
@tashasabatini

Follow me on Twitter @tasha_sabatini

I'm on Tumblr as well under Tasha Sabatini! Give it a look!

Feel free to contact me using any of these platforms.

Author Bio

Tasha Sabatini, age just 16. Adventure ambassador of the natural world. An advocate of outdoor recreation, or as she would prefer to call it, adventuring. Growing up in Northwest Pennsylvania; running barefooted through fields and woods. Her environment cultivating her love for the outdoors is what has driven her to write Primal Reconnection; with hopes of reconnecting individuals with their inner primal roots.

Dictionary Credits:

Oxford Dictionaries | Our Story, Products, Technology, and ..." N.p., n.d. Web.

43709843R00055